B… …Bluth

Rock-a-Doodle

Story written by Neil Morris

Hippo Books
Scholastic Publications Limited
London

Scholastic Publications Ltd.,
10 Earlham Street, London WC2H 9RX, UK

Scholastic Inc.,
730 Broadway, New York, NY 10003, USA

Scholastic Canada Ltd.,
123 Newkirk Road, Richmond Hill,
Ontario L4C 3G5, Canada

Ashton Scholastic Pty. Ltd.,
P O Box 579, Gosford, New South Wales,
Australia

Ashton Scholastic Pty Ltd.,
Private Bag 1, Penrose, Auckland
New Zealand

First published by Scholastic Publications Ltd., 1991

ISBN 0 590 76517 5

Typeset by Keyline Graphics, London NW6
Made and printed in Spain
by Mateu Cromo, Madrid

Edmond sat up in bed as his mother read him the story in his picture book. It was called *The Story of Chanticleer*, and Edmond loved it.

Chanticleer was a fun-loving rooster, popular with all the other animals in the farmyard. Each morning everyone awoke to his "cock-a-doodle-doo". In fact, the animals all believed that it was Chanticleer's wonderful voice that made the sun come up each day.

But early one morning, while it was still dark and Chanticleer was waiting till it was time to crow, a mysterious stranger arrived. He was a strong fighting cock with shining black and white feathers, and he went straight for Chanticleer. There was a ferocious battle. The intruder had greater strength, but Chanticleer had a braver heart. When the battle was over, it was Chanticleer who had won. And yet at the same time he had lost, for there had been no time to crow and now the sun was peeping over the hillside.

When the rooster saw the sunlight, it almost broke his heart. Perhaps it wasn't his voice that made the sun rise after all? The animals whispered among themselves. "Look, it's coming up without him!" quacked a dumbfounded duck.

"He's a phoney," grunted a pig.

"Hey, everybody, cock-a-doodle-doo! Ha-ha!" laughed Snipes the magpie.

Chanticleer walked sadly away. As he left the farm, the sun went in and storm clouds gathered. Soon lightning flashed and rain fell in torrents.

"Who's that, Mum?" asked Edmond, pointing to an owl in his book.

"That's the Grand Duke," the little boy's mother replied, "ruler of the night creatures. He sent that mean fighting cock to the farm."

"But why?" asked Edmond.

"Because he didn't like the rooster doing all that crowing and bringing up the sun. Like most owls, he likes the darkness and the rain."

"I'm not afraid of the dark," Edmond said proudly. At that moment the door flew open, revealing a rain-soaked figure. Mother and son were startled, but it was only Edmond's father. "If the rain doesn't let up soon," he said, "we'll all be floating down the river. I must get the animals into the barn. I'll get the boys to help."

"Me too!" shouted Edmond.

"You stop right there," his mother said firmly. "Dad meant the big boys, your brothers. Now you stay here, I'll be right back."

Edmond opened his book at the page where Chanticleer walked away in the rain. Then he looked at the downpour outside. "What if he never comes back?" he whispered to himself. "Chanticleer!" he yelled at the top of his voice. Edmond got out of bed and went to the window. He opened it, and gazed into the dark, dark night. "Chanticleer!" he called again. Suddenly, lightning struck a tree outside the window. A huge branch exploded into the room, knocking Edmond onto the floor, where he lay unconscious for several minutes.

When he came to, Edmond saw a shadowy figure at the window. "Who . . . who are you?" he stammered.

"You put your finger in the Duke's face . . . remember?" came the reply. It was the evil owl. "And then you have the nerve to call that bird back here," the Grand Duke went on. "And for what? Just so he can spoil this beautiful stormy darkness with his terrible crowing!" The giant owl swooped towards the little boy.

"Help! Help!" cried Edmond.

"My, what a fuss," laughed the owl. "Why don't you just let me eat you and have done with it?" He lunged at Edmond. "But little boys are so difficult to eat. Kittens are much more digestible." With that, the Grand Duke shot a thunderous bolt of light at Edmond. There was an enormous flash, and Edmond's pyjamas were left in an empty heap on the floor. A few moments later, a tiny white kitten peeped through the collar. The Grand Duke roared with laughter.

But he soon stopped when Patou, the kind old farm dog, leapt through the window and sank his teeth into the owl's fat leg.

While Patou fought with the owl, Edmond the kitten struggled to pick up a heavy torch. At last he switched it on and pointed it at the Grand Duke. When the beam hit the owl's eyes, he screamed and shot out of the window like a cannonball. "Hey, that torch was quick thinkin'," laughed Patou, trying to tie his shoelaces. "I'd have whopped him if I'd had my shoes tied. You know, tyin' shoes is harder than dry dogfood!"

Edmond held out his hand to help Patou with his laces, but it wasn't a hand, it was a paw! "Jeepers, I'm all furry!" cried Edmond, feeling the long whiskers on his face.

"Well, kittens are furry," said Patou, looking puzzled.

"But I'm a little boy," protested Edmond. Slowly he turned to face the mirror, and looked at his reflection in disbelief. "I'm a cat," he gasped, "he turned me into a cat."

Suddenly, Edmond realized he wasn't wearing anything, so he quickly put on the clothes his Davy Crocket doll was wearing.

At that moment a tiny voice called for Patou. "I'm in here," barked the dog. And to Edmond's amazement, in from the storm came a mouse, a magpie, and assorted pigs, rabbits, chickens and ducks. Edmond put on his biggest kitten's voice. "If Chanticleer doesn't come back and crow, the sun will never shine again," he said. "The rain will keep falling, and the water will get higher and higher, till we all drown."

"That's why we have to get to the city," said Patou. "We've got to find Chanti and apologize."

"I know where the city is," Edmond said proudly. "I've been there lots of times . . . as a boy," he added sadly. Just then water began to gush into the room. Edmond jumped into a toybox, and Patou swam towards him. As the toybox was swept away, Peepers the mouse and Snipes the magpie managed to pull themselves aboard. The rest of the animals sat on Edmond's bed, with the torch to guard against the owls. Outside in the storm-driven flood waters, Edmond and his friends went sailing past half-submerged houses and telegraph poles. As they struggled to steer the box, they were attacked by a squadron of owls, led by Hunch, the Grand Duke's useless nephew.

Patou tried to shut the lid of the box, as the owls closed in.
"I got you, kitty!" Hunch howled. This infuriated Edmond, who suddenly had an idea. There was a toy camera in the box, and Edmond told Peepers of his plan. When the owls flew near, the mouse popped up and pressed the button. FLASH!!! She aimed the flashbulb straight at their eyes. Hunch crashed and the other owls flew away.

Patou slammed the lid closed again, just as the toybox disappeared into the black hole of a large water pipe. Hunch reported all this to his uncle. "I really got 'em," he lied. "No more kitty, sir. We sucked 'em into an adequate pipe."

"A what?" asked a puzzled Grand Duke.

"That's what the sign said," Hunch babbled. "Danger – adequate pipe."

The Duke zapped his nephew with a magic blast. "Imbecile!" he bellowed. "That's not an adequate pipe, it's an aqueduct pipe. It leads straight into the city!"

At that moment the four friends in the toybox had no idea where they were heading. And Snipes was starting to go crazy. "He'th clauthtrophobic," lisped Peepers. "Teeny-weeny platheth make him nervouth." Snipes was using his beak to get out, but the holes he was making were letting water in!

Just in time, the box plunged out of the pipe into a tank below. It smashed open, and the inmates climbed aboard a floating barrel. Looking up, they saw the city skyline.

"Wow!" cried Snipes.

"It'th tho beautiful!" added Peepers.

"Now all we have to do is find Chanticleer," said Patou, "and that'll be like hunting for a needle in a haystack."

As the four friends wandered through the big city, full of bright lights and honking horns, they didn't realize how close they were to finding Chanticleer. If they had only listened, they would have heard his wonderful voice coming from every jukebox and record shop. And if they had only looked, they would have recognized his face on the poster on every street corner.

The posters advertised concerts by "the King". And who was "the King"? Why, Chanticleer, of course! After leaving the farm, he had come to the city, where he was discovered by the famous music and movie manager, Pinky, the fox. And now he was the biggest name in show business, playing to a packed house at Pinky's Palace.

But Chanticleer's friends had no idea that he was a big star. They sat on the kerb in front of Pinky's Palace, and still didn't realize! And unknown to them they faced a great danger. High above the city, Hunch was searching for them. Suddenly he spotted them through his binoculars and zoomed in for a closer look. Luckily, he missed his target and crash-landed in an alleyway.

Meanwhile, Edmond was busy teaching Patou to tie his laces, Snipes was depressed, and Peepers was wondering where they should try next. Suddenly she looked up and at last saw the giant model of the King playing his guitar. "Jumping Jehothaphat!" she cried "It'th him!"

The truth finally dawned. Now all they had to do was get Chanticleer back to the farm to crow the sun up: then surely the rain would stop. Edmond ran to a phone box to ring his friends on the farm. "We're running out of time," Stuey the pig wailed, as water rose around him. "We need Chanti, quick!"

Meanwhile Chanticleer's manager was speaking to the Grand Duke, who phoned to warn him that a cat, a dog, a bird, and a mouse were aiming to take the King back to the farm. Pinky told Goldie, a beautiful pheasant in the King's chorus, to watch out for the four. He persuaded her that the King was lonely and needed a friend. "But watch out for that bad little kitty," the fat manager warned her through clouds of cigar smoke, "he wants to steal the King away, and you don't want that do you?"

But the four friends had already managed to get into Pinky's Palace disguised as penguins. When the show started, the King stood on the deck of a sunken ship in a pretend underwater scene. His superb voice filled the Palace. But Edmond scarcely listened: he was busy writing a letter, which he passed to the others to sign too. Snipes read it out: "Dear Chanticleer, We're sorry, please come home, help, we need you! Signed, your friends."

Edmond folded the letter into a paper plane and launched it towards the stage. Unfortunately, it was caught by one of the mechanical sharks whizzing round the stage, so the four of them headed backstage to rescue it. They quickly dressed as lobsters and Edmond climbed onto a shark and dislodged the letter, which floated into the King's hand. But just then, Goldie the pheasant made her entrance and plucked the letter from the King's grasp, as she smacked him a kiss on the beak.

And that night it seemed that although Goldie was only supposed to fall in love with Chanticleer, she was falling in love for real. And Chanticleer? Why, he had almost forgotten about his friends on the farm.

The next day, Edmond and his friends went to Pinky's film studios, where Goldie and Chanticleer were making a film together. Edmond went straight to Goldie's dressing room to beg her to give Chanticleer the letter, but it was no good.

"You're that bad little kitty!" Goldie said, and screamed at the top of her pheasant's voice. This alerted a squad of bouncers, who quickly captured Edmond, rounded up his friends, and locked them all up in Pinky's caravan.

But later, on Pinky's film set, Goldie felt guilty about what she had done. She gave Edmond's letter to the King. When Chanticleer read it, he decided at once to help his old friends, who at that moment were trying to fight off Hunch. He had spotted the bouncers taking them to the caravan, and had dived into attack. Chanticleer didn't know this, but he had to escape from Pinky! He revved up his motorbike and shot out of the studio with Goldie. They didn't get very far, for Pinky's trailer was parked right outside the studio doors.

Chanticleer crashed straight into the trailer and was promptly knocked out by Patou, who was aiming to hit Hunch at the time! The friends took off at once with Chanticleer and Goldie in Pinky's pink Cadillac. Pinky and his army of guards ran for the nearest cars, trucks and even golf cart. The chase was on!

Meanwhile, Hunch was climbing along the trailer which was attached to the Cadillac. He had to be stopped! Peepers crawled out to free the trailer, but was accidentally knocked back with it. Her friends were horrified and turned back to get her. Pinky and his followers swerved to avoid them, and the Caddy came to a sudden halt at a tall water tower.

Everyone jumped out of the car and started to climb the tower. The guards clambered after them, but at the top of the tower the friends were whisked away by Pinky's pink helicopter. But who was flying it? None other than little Peepers, who wasn't hurt and had commandeered the machine.

"Come back with my 'copter!" bawled the furious Pinky, as the helicopter flew off – rather unsteadily – into the distance. Where were they heading? Back to the farm, of course.

At the farm the Grand Duke was sharpening a carving knife, looking forward to a pork dinner. Suddenly there was the deafening swoosh of helicopter blades. But pilot Peepers was having to fight off Hunch, who yet again had turned up to do damage. "Oh no," cried the mouse, "the'th going down! Abandon thip!" There was a loud crash. The helicopter certainly was down. But the friends were all safe.

The bump even brought Chanticleer round. "Hey, is it time for the show?" he asked. "Show me the stage . . . gimme that mike!"

"Chanti, you're home," said Patou. "You've got to crow, and you've got to crow now."

"I can't . . . I don't know if I ever could," replied the rooster.

"It's your job to bring up the sun!" cried Edmond.

"It hathn't thined thinth you left," added Peepers.

At that Chanticleer threw his head back, puffed out his chest and tried to crow. But all that came out was a muffled squawk. "It's no use," he said sadly. "All I can do now is sing the blues."

"But we don't want the King," cried Edmond, "we want Chanticleer. Come on, everybody. Chanticleer . . . Chanticleer. . .", he chanted until he was stopped by a horrible scream.

"Silence!!!" It was the Grand Duke, swollen to an enormous size and surging with power. The evil owl sent Edmond a magic blast, which picked him up and tossed him on a hill, where he lay motionless.

Slowly all the other animals took up the chant. "Chanticleer . . . Chanticleer . . . Chanticleer. . ."

"Shut up, fools!" the Duke screamed in rage. With that, he grew into a mighty tornado. The winds blew and the rains grew stronger. Without Chanticleer's crow, the Duke's magic was unstoppable!

Everyone looked at Chanticleer. Suddenly he flew up into the air, opened his beak and crowed a crow to reach the stars: "Cock-a-doodle-DOO!!!"

A brilliant beam of sunlight came slowly over the hill. It made straight for the Grand Duke, who quickly shrank to a size smaller than a mouse. The owl disappeared into the distance, chased by Hunch, who was now much bigger than his evil uncle!

More rays burned through the clouds, and soon the farm was bathed in beautiful sunlight. The rain stopped and the flood waters went down. A sunbeam warmed the spot where Edmond lay. His friends drew back in amazement as the kitten slowly changed back into a boy.

When Edmond woke up, he was lying in bed, with his mother at his side. He picked up the book and saw his hands. "Mum, I'm not furry any more," he cried. "I'm a boy!" And he told her all about his adventures.

His mother smiled as she left the room, "It's only a storybook," she reminded him. But Edmond knew better and was delighted to hear a familiar sound: "Cock-a-doodle-doo!" It was Chanticleer, rocking around the farmyard. Edmond laughed. "Chanticleer!" he shouted, and leapt out of bed to join all his friends outside.